MW01530519

TABLE OF CONTENTS

Cover Art by
Matthew Archambault

Black & White Illustrations by
Ken Landgraf

EDCON

Publishing Group

Copyright © 2006
AV Concepts Corporation
Edcon Publishing Group

Printed in U.S.A.
ISBN# 1-55576-388-X

COMMUNICATION SKILLS

COMMUNICATION SKILLS

LISTENING SKILLS & NON-VERBAL COMMUNICATION

A musical toy –

A baby recognizing his own sounds –

The buzzing of a bee –

COMMUNICATION SKILLS

The start-up of a
motorcycle's engine –

The sound of a
marching band –

The piano in
kindergarten class.

COMMUNICATION SKILLS

Children learn how to appreciate sounds, however, children are seldom taught how to listen.

They learn how to speak at an early age –

...and to read –

...and to write.

Some children rely more on listening comprehension than on reading. In fact, some say that 80% of all learning is achieved by listening.

Listening skills form the base for classroom learning as well as teacher-student interaction.

COMMUNICATION SKILLS

Listening is a fast, easy way to acquire knowledge.

You can listen to a CD while engaged in another activity.

COMMUNICATION SKILLS

When we are listening, we must become aware of the NON-VERBAL signs we are SENDING and RECEIVING. We must be certain we are receiving concrete words that don't require a great deal of interpretation. Our vocabulary must include words that describe our feelings, emotions, and actions. The interpretation of these "feelings" words will determine how we think about ourselves.

"Yeah, all that sounds great, but when Mr. Cox talks, I listen for a while, then my mind seems to drift. I just can't stay awake."

COMMUNICATION SKILLS

This is typical for most of us. The mental drifting exists because the thinking process is twice as fast as the speaking process. As listeners, we must try extra hard to use this spare mental time.

As listeners, we must guard against built-in biases and stereotypes; beliefs about race and sex can affect how we interpret what we hear.

ACTIVE LISTENERS use their spare mental time in three ways. They

1. **THINK AHEAD OF THE SPEAKER.**
2. **REVIEW THE CENTRAL THEME.**
3. **EVALUATE WHAT IS HEARD.**

Practicing the rules of ACTIVE LISTENING will make us better speakers. As speakers, we must remember to use repetition, humor, and suspense, as well as vary our speaking tone. Psychologists tell us that a listener's attention span is only 25 seconds. This makes the need for variety and repetition by speakers extremely important. The speaker must be aware of his audience's verbal level of development. Comprehension levels vary greatly among adults, children, and even social classes.

Listeners must strive to retain the basic facts. Often, short notes help us to use spare listening time and reinforce retention of information. These notes can be used as an aid to interpret what the speaker said.

The students at Rolling Hills High School love Miss Ryder, the school's counselor. She conveys to the students that she's very interested in them by NON-VERBAL COMMUNICATION, also known as body language. Her attending behavior – a warm smile, body slightly bent forward in her seat, her use of hand gestures, and the way she makes eye contact, leaves no barrier between her and the student.

"Miss Ryder," said Johnny, "I'm having a lot of trouble in French class. No matter how hard I study, I seem to fail. I just don't know what to do."

Miss Ryder replied, "John, you seem to feel frustrated because you're not passing, and don't know where to turn. Perhaps we can design a plan for you."

"That sounds great! Miss Ryder, maybe I'll pass French after all."

This counselor was listening to the student. She picked up on the emotional despair expressed by the student and reflected this in her reply, thus demonstrating that she heard and understood.

"Kathy, I don't know why you're complaining. I told you at the beginning of the semester you were going to fail," said Jim.

COMMUNICATION SKILLS

When we respond in a manner that does not demonstrate understanding, we are actually discouraging further conversation and often make our listener angry.

Over a period of time our verbal expressions become automatic. A tape recorder is an effective way to study our speaking and listening habits. By recording conversations with others, we can determine the areas needing improvement. The tape recorder can also be a teaching tool for children to become aware of their listening and responding patterns. After each recording session, we should play back the recording and analyze it for patterns and habits that might need correcting.

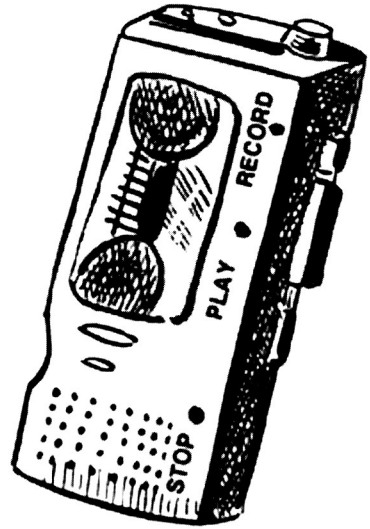

Developing any skill requires continuous practice, whether it's shooting a basketball or listening.

Each of us must begin today to improve these skills. Perhaps tomorrow we'll be better listeners.

COMMUNICATION SKILLS

LISTENING SKILLS & NON-VERBAL COMMUNICATION

COMPLETE THE SENTENCES
Fill in the blanks in the following sentences using the correct words from the box below.

central theme	practice	speaking tone
vocabulary	25 seconds	think ahead
notes	mental drifting	knowledge
listening	evaluate	retain

1. _____exists because the thinking process is twice as fast as the speaking process.

2. 80% of all learning is achieved by _____.

3. Listening is an easy way to acquire _____.

4. Psychologists tell us that a listener's attention span is only _____.

5. Active listeners _____ of the speaker, review the_____, and _____what is heard.

6. To improve the skill of listening, we must _____.

7. Listeners must strive to _____ basic facts.

8. To help retain the basic facts and reinforce retention, listeners can rely on _____.

9. When speaking, it is important to vary our _____.

10. Our _____ must include words that describe our feelings, emotions, and actions.

Answers can be found on page 53.

COMMUNICATION SKILLS

LISTENING SKILLS & NON-VERBAL COMMUNICATION

MATCHING

Match the word(s) in Column A to the correct definition in Column B.

Column A	Column B
_____1. mental drifting	a. a smile
_____2. slouching	b. teaching tool
_____3. facial expression	c. hand gestures
_____4. tape recorder	d. the result of not using spare mental time
_____5. body language	e. non-verbal sign

TRUE (T) or FALSE (F)

_____ 1. Non-verbal communication is communication without sound.

_____ 2. It's important to become aware of the non-verbal signs we send and receive.

_____ 3. A listener's attention span is approximately 3 minutes.

_____ 4. It is important to maintain eye contact when speaking.

_____ 5. 80% of all learning is achieved by listening.

Answers can be found on page 53.

PROBLEM
SOLVING

PROBLEM SOLVING

Remember your first problems and how you solved them? Like riding the big playground horse – or that first adventure on the big slide? Often, our friends were there to help us and, of course, we only needed one successful slide for us to forget all of our problems.
At school we began to develop more difficult problems. We had to learn to get along with our counselors, teachers, and other students.
As we matured and developed, we learned that problems are common to everyone.

HAVE A PROBLEM
CAN YOU HELP ME ?

Some students are able to identify a problem quickly, have confidence in solving the problem, and follow problem-solving procedures that lead to success.
Others, who don't understand problem-solving procedures, can't see the solutions –

PROBLEM SOLVING

no matter how hard they look. They become paralyzed by a problem, lose control, and the ability for them to solve problems is diminished.

Much of our success in solving problems is related to our personal belief that we can solve problems. If we believe and have confidence in ourselves, we have a far greater chance of being successful.

If we think logically, plan our strategies effectively, then all the pieces will fit together like a jigsaw puzzle.

Many people assume that we learn problem-solving skills from our parents or from our teachers. In most cases, our parents and teachers TELL US what to do and neglect to TEACH US the problem-solving skills. For example,

PROBLEM SOLVING

Peggy has just been informed that she must select her courses for next year. She can still hear Miss Kahn reviewing the problem-solving process:

"Now, class, always remember that problem solving consists of a series of skills rather than just one specific skill."

RECOGNIZE PROBLEMS

"First, you must have the ability to recognize a problem.

IDENTIFY THE SPECIFIC PROBLEM

"Then, you must be able to identify the specific problem. Often, it helps if you can write the problem down and analyze it – separate the facts from the opinions.

PROBLEM SOLVING

RESEARCH THE PROBLEM

"Research your problem, gather data, and state a step-by-step approach that will lead to a solution. This is what many researchers call MEANS ENDS THINKING – or the ability to logically establish a plan to solve a problem and the ability to enact the plan.

EVALUATE THE CONSEQUENCES

"Finally, we must determine how our proposed solution will affect others and how it will affect us. Is cheating on a test the most effective solution? How would this action affect us? How would it affect our friends?

"Social adjustment is directly related to how effectively we can generate solutions for our daily problems. Adjustment during adulthood is directly related to how well we learned to solve problems as a youth.

PROBLEM SOLVING

NOTHING
FLOP
FIZZLE
FORGET IT

"Poor problem solvers seem to have broken solution generators, so it's important for all of us to make sure our solution generator is in good working order."

Before we return to Peggy's problem, let's take a few minutes to write down the following basic problem-solving facts:

1. PROBLEMS ARE NORMAL AND COMMON

2. IDENTIFY AND DEFINE THE PROBLEM

3. GATHER INFORMATION

4. SEPARATE FACT FROM OPINION

5. ESTABLISH A REALISTIC SOLUTION

6. GENERATE ALTERNATIVE SOLUTIONS

7. IDENTIFY THE CONSEQUENCES

8. INITIATE AN ACTION PLAN

PROBLEM SOLVING

Now let's practice identifying problems. On the lines below, write down your solution(s) to each of the following problems.

Problem # 1 Ready to head to work one very cold winter morning, you go to your car only to find that there's ice on your windshield.

Solution _____

_____

Alternative

Solution _____

_____

Problem # 2 You see a snake slithering in the grass in your backyard.

Solution _____

_____

Alternative

Solution _____

_____

Problem # 3 You go outside one snowy morning to find that a snow plow has left a pile of snow at the end of your driveway, and you can't get your car out.

Solution _____

_____

Alternative

Solution _____

Now, let's go over your remedies.

Problem # 1	Ice has accumulated on your windshield.
Solution	Scrape the ice off your windshield.
Alternative Solution	Turn on your car's defroster and wait for the windshield to clear.

Problem # 2	You see a snake in the grass.
Solution	Carefully remove the snake from your yard.
Alternative Solution	Go indoors and wait for the snake to leave your yard.

Problem # 3	A snow plow has blocked your driveway with snow.
Solution	Shovel the snow away.
Alternative Solution	Stay home – don't plan to leave the driveway.

The solutions to the above problems may vary depending on your perspective or how you look at things. The important thing is that you learn to identify problems, generate solutions, and begin to think about how these solutions will affect us and those around us.

PROBLEM SOLVING

Now, let's practice identifying fact from opinion. Remember that WHAT YOU SEE is FACT, and WHAT YOU THINK YOU SEE is an OPINION.

Scenario 1:   A young man is sitting at a drum set. A bright light is shining on him.
Is this a fact or an opinion?

Please check.   _____   _____
                                FACT   OPINION

Scenario 2:   He's playing the drums and it makes him hot.
Is this a fact or an opinion?

Please check.   _____   _____
                                FACT   OPINION

Scenario 3:   Alice's hands are covered with a brown substance. Her hair is long, and she is wearing a blue shirt.
Is this a fact or an opinion?

Please check.   _____   _____
                                FACT   OPINION

Answers
#1 is fact
#2 is opinion
#3 is fact

However, don't you wonder what Alice had been doing?

If you said that it looked as though Alice had been eating a large chocolate bar and it had melted in her hands, you would be stating an opinion, for you really don't know.

The **fact** is, as some of you may have guessed, is that Alice had been working with clay in art class.

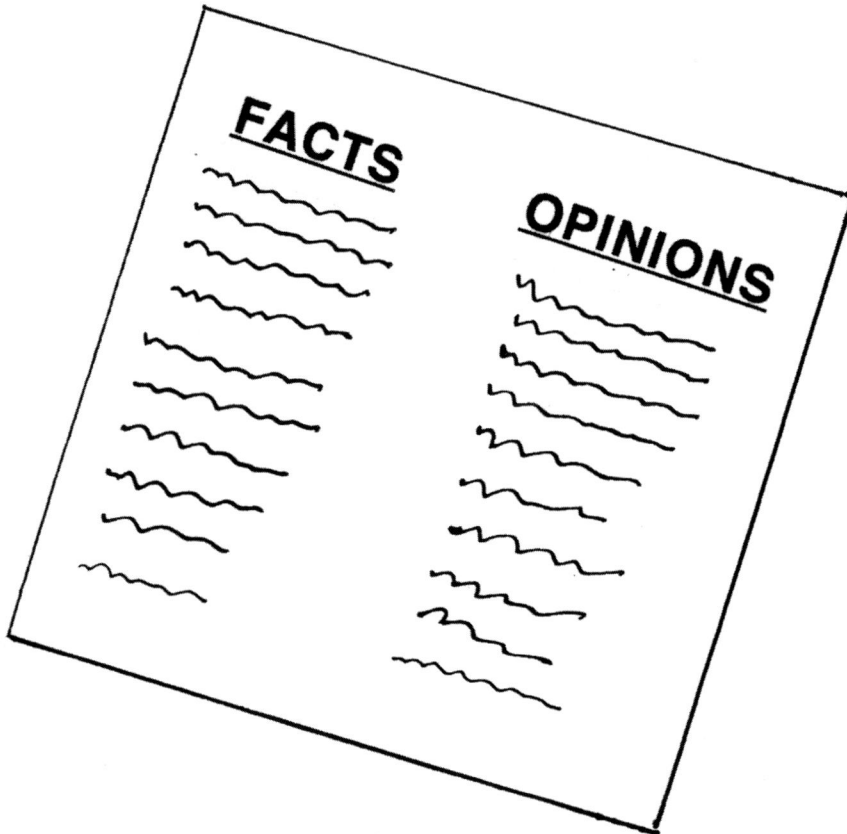

FACTS

OPINIONS

As you have learned, separating fact from opinion is a very important problem-solving skill. To practice this skill, some people like to make a list of FACTS in one column and OPINIONS in another. This list is extremely important for gathering and analyzing data for problem solving and decision making. With a little practice, you'll be an expert!

PROBLEM SOLVING

Now, let's return to our friend Peggy. Remember that her problem was selecting courses for next year? She must gather information from her school's course catalog, from her friends, parents, and school counselor. She must carefully separate fact from opinion, make decisions, propose possible solutions, and think about the consequences of her decisions.
She will double-check the course catalog, discuss her decision with her friends, parents, and school counselor, and create an action plan.

Making important decisions gives you confidence and increases your problem-solving ability. But, like all skills, those associated with problem solving take a lot of practice. The more you practice, the better you'll become at problem solving. So start practicing today!

SENTENCE COMPLETION
Use the words in the box to complete the sentences below.

recognize	fact
practice	can
series	opinion

1. Success in solving problems is related to personal belief that we _____ solve problems.

2. Problem solving consists of a _____ of skills rather than one specific skill.

3. The first step in problem solving is to _____ and identify the specific problem.

4. Separating _____ from _____ is a necessary problem-solving skill.

5. Like most skills, problem-solving skills increase with _____.

Answers can be found on page 54

PROBLEM SOLVING

TRUE (T) or FALSE (F)

_____ 1. Problems are normal and common.

_____ 2. First you must identify and define the problem.

_____ 3. The second step is to gather information.

_____ 4. Facts must be separated from opinions.

_____ 5. In solving a problem, you must establish a realistic plan.

_____ 6. Generate alternative solutions for each problem.

_____ 7. Identify the consequences of each solution.

_____ 8. Initiate an action plan.

Answers can be found on page 54

GETTING A JOB

GETTING A JOB

Bob had just finished his painting. "You know," said Bob, "I could work on art projects for the rest of my life. Time really flies when you're having fun."

Bob's friend Jerry was forming a bowl on the pottery wheel. "Yeah, watching a lump of clay turning into a beautiful pot is just *fantastic!*" answered Jerry.

Bob said, "But next month, when we graduate, then what are we going to do?"

"I guess we'll have to find jobs," answered Jerry. "You got a job lined up, Bob?"

"No," replied Bob, "but I'm working on it. I'm learning how to go about getting a job."

"Well, working with clay is fun, and I think it's a great leisure-time activity, but I guess I've got to get a job paying *real* money," said Jerry.

* * * * *

GETTING A JOB

Jerry and Bob are typical high school students. They're a little scared about going out into the world and finding a job. But, it's not really that scary. Getting a job will help you buy things you like –

or things you need.

Getting a job can be divided into 3 separate parts:

> 1. **SELF-KNOWLEDGE**
> 2. **THE JOB SEARCH**
> 3. **THE INTERVIEW**

Let's look at number 1. The easiest way to learn about yourself is to make a list of your likes and dislikes, your education, and your work experiences. Collect the information in a job folder. Be sure to include all your activities such as soccer, swimming, basketball, community or volunteer activities. And don't forget to include the time you spent on your art projects.

Think about the school subjects and activities you like and dislike. Talk to your friends and teachers and have them name two of your strongest and two of your weakest traits. List any specialized training you received at a local college, a trade school, or night school.

Now, let's look at number 2. The job search requires collecting information from many sources such as

the newspaper –

the State Employment Office –

and a visit to your local post office or federal building to inquire about job opportunities, and to pick up a listing of the latest civil service jobs. Even if you don't qualify for some of these jobs now, you might in the future.

Pick up some career flyers from your high school counselor or job placement counselor.

Finally, let's examine number 3. Prior to your first interview, review the information in your folder. Often, when you look at all the lists and piece them together, you get a pattern or picture of yourself. Now, think about the type of work situation you are interested in.

Would you like to work in an office?

Or outside doing construction?

With both feet on the ground?

Or high up in the air?

Knowing the type of work and working conditions you are seeking will save you a great deal of time and effort.

GETTING A JOB

Now, remember sources for finding a job:

1. **LOCAL NEWSPAPER**
2. **STATE EMPLOYMENT OFFICE**
3. **CIVIL SERVICE OFFICE**
4. **PLACEMENT COUNSELOR**

The job interview will make you or break you. Before you go, review your job folder, go over your resumé, and think about what you are going to say. Then, check your appearance:

1. **USE PLENTY OF SOAP AND WATER**
2. **SELECT YOUR FINEST CLOTHES**
3. **COMB YOUR HAIR**
4. **MAKE SURE YOU LOOK NEAT AND CLEAN**

I'm going to leave early and make sure I'm there on time, thought Rick.

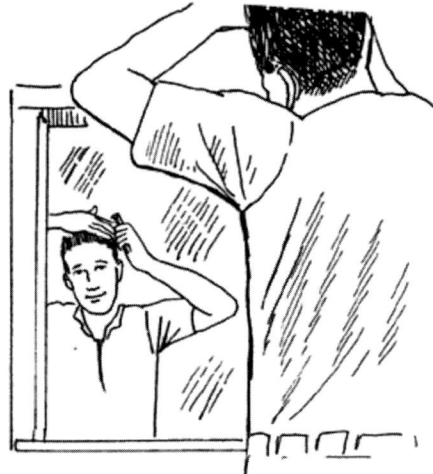

I'm lucky that I could borrow this car. If I get this job, I'll have to take a bus or share a ride with a fellow worker.

Rick arrived at his destination. *Wow. I'm really too early for my interview,* he thought. *I think I'll stop by another company's personnel office and see if they have any job openings.*

Good thinking, Rick. Sometimes cold calls produce results. That company may not have an opening right now, but maybe they will later. They might know of other companies that are hiring.
Be sure to seek out the personnel director – don't ask employees about a job. And, above all, don't be discouraged if you're not hired right away. These days, good jobs are hard to find – so you are likely to be rejected several times.
When you go to the job interview, remember these BEES:

> 1. **BEE EARLY**
> 2. **BEE PATIENT**
> 3. **BEE INTERESTED**
> 4. **BEE FRIENDLY**
> 5. **BEE HONEST**

And remember these DON'TS:

> 1. **DON'T CHEW GUM**
> 2. **DON'T SMOKE**
> 3. **DON'T BE A WISE GUY**
> 4. **DON'T HAVE A BAD ATTITUDE**

GETTING A JOB

"Jerry," said Bob, "I'm going to look for a nice easy job that requires creative talent and pays *lots* of money."

"Bob, if you find a job like that, let me know," replied Jerry, "that is, as long as I don't have to get my hands dirty."

GETTING A JOB

SENTENCE COMPLETION
Use the words in the box to complete the sentences below.

interests	income	yourself
newspapers	resumé	friends
interview	search	benefits

1. Before you begin to look for a job, you should collect as much information about _____ as possible.

2. This must include your _____ such as math, English, working indoors or outdoors.

3. As you begin your job _____, you must look in _____ and talk to _____ to determine what jobs are available in your area.

4. Before you go for an _____, you must prepare a _____, which will list your education, work experience, and provide a list of references.

5. At the interview, you will learn how much _____ you will make as well as the _____ you will receive.

Alfonso is going for an interview tomorrow. His teacher told him to remember to be early, be interested, and be friendly. List some other things that he should remember.

1.

2.

3.

4.

5.

Answers can be found on page 55.

GETTING A JOB

JOB PARTS
Getting a job is divided into three (3) separate parts. Can you name them?

1. _____

2. _____

3. _____

Learn about yourself by creating a job folder.
Make a list of your likes and dislikes.

I LIKE	I DON'T LIKE
_____	_____
_____	_____
_____	_____
_____	_____
_____	_____

On a separate sheet of paper, create a resumé. List your educational background, any work experience, and your hobbies and interests. Use this space to make notes.

Education: (List all schools, colleges, trade schools, etc.)

Sports/Hobbies/Community Service/Volunteer Work (List all your activities)

Answers can be found on page 55.

THE JOB SEARCH

1. **The job search requires collecting information from various sources. Where can some of this information be found?**

2. **What should you do before going to a job interview?**

3. **Put a check next to the things you should NOT do during your interview.**

___Smile	___Be patient
___Chew Gum	___Yawn
___Answer your cell phone	___Tell a bad joke
___Be honest	___Look discouraged
___Bite your fingernails	___Comb your hair
___Be friendly	___Put on lipstick
___Smoke	___Be a wise guy
___Have a bad attitude	___Be calm
___Be interested	___Be courteous

Answers can be found on page 55.

KEEPING A JOB

"Jerry. . .you're fired!"

"We just don't need you anymore."

"Yes, Alvin, you're fired! Pick up your check and be on your way."

* * * * *

KEEPING A JOB

For some of us, getting a job is easy, but keeping it is a different story. Take the case of Jerry Light, for instance.

"Jerry began working for me about two months ago," said Mr. Scott, owner of a furniture store. "He was a nice boy, neatly dressed, and real friendly. His art teacher was a personal friend of mine. She said he was well-liked by his classmates. So, I hired Jerry and assigned him several jobs around the store.
"At first he was a willing worker. But after about a week, the trouble started. Jerry began showing up late for work.

"He abused his break time and never returned from lunch on time.

"One day I had to get to the bank before it closed and I needed the back storage area cleaned for a new shipment of lamps due to arrive in the morning.
"I carefully explained to Jerry exactly what needed to be done and why it was so important.
I just had to get to the bank before 3:00!

"When I returned from the bank and found that the storage area had not been cleaned, I was furious! I'd had it with Jerry. He was not responsible, dependable, nor a willing worker.

"Just the day before, my warehouse foreman called to tell me about Dave, a boy he had hired. He had a big job to do at the loading dock and he needed some extra help.

"No one had recommended this boy, and his appearance made him look like a hippie. But, my foreman took a chance. He gave Dave some jobs to do, then left to make some deliveries. "Well, the boy worked so hard that when he finished his assignments, he started another job. This shows initiative and responsibility.

KEEPING A JOB

"Dave is the type of employee I need to make my business grow. So, we gave Dave a raise. . .and fired Jerry."

* * * * *

Now, let's tell the story of Sarah Note.

Sarah's been working in the music store for about two weeks now. She says she likes the job. She has fun waiting on customers and keeping the shelves stocked. She likes her boss, Mr. Russell. She says he's nice – and easy to work for. Sometimes she gets tired of standing all day, but she knows that's part of the job.

Sarah hears the door chime which alerts her that a customer has entered the store. Turning around, she sees her friends Susan and Nancy. Sarah waves to her friends. Her friends wave back. Susan walks over to check out some CD's, while Nancy joins her friend Sarah.

Sarah pulls Nancy aside, out of earshot of the other customers in the store, and whispers, "Listen. . .don't buy anything in this store – the prices are too high. Go down the street to the other music store. You'll get a much better deal."

Nancy is surprised to hear this, but she takes Sarah's advice and leaves the store with Susan.

After her friends left the store, Sarah returned to work and thought of how nice it would be to have a couple of the latest CD's. *No one will ever know*, thought Sarah. Just as Sarah was putting the CD's into her purse behind the counter,

Shoplifters will be Prosecuted

Mr. Russell came up behind her. Pointing to a sign on the wall, he reminds Sarah that stealing is a serious crime.
Sarah pays for the tapes, but the damage has already been done. Mr. Russell cannot trust her.

Two of the most important traits an employee can have are

1. **LOYALTY**
2. **HONESTY**

KEEPING A JOB

"If I'm going to stay in business, I'm going to need employees I can trust – and who are loyal to me. Sarah was not – so I had to fire her."

Now, let me tell you the story of Alvin Klok.

Mr. Sanders, Alvin's boss, hears the store's door open and wonders why Alvin isn't there to wait on customers.

Alvin is engaged in his favorite pastime – reading car magazines – but he reluctantly throws down the magazine and strolls to the front of the store to wait on a customer.

Alvin attempts to comb his hair with his hand and wonders why Mr. Sanders doesn't wait on this customer. Alvin's appearance and attitude are quickly observed by the customer who feels uneasy, and unwelcome, and leaves the store.

Let's look at some of the common-sense items needed to keep a job. You must be

1. **RESPONSIBLE**
2. **DEPENDABLE**
3. **A WILLING WORKER**
4. **LOYAL**
5. **HONEST**
6. **HAVE A GOOD ATTITUDE**
7. **LISTEN TO INSTRUCTIONS**
8. **FOLLOW DIRECTIONS**
9. **TAKE THE INITIATIVE**

"I fired Alvin because he chased customers away," said Mr. Sanders. "He was indifferent and had a chip on his shoulder– just a bad attitude."

KEEPING A JOB

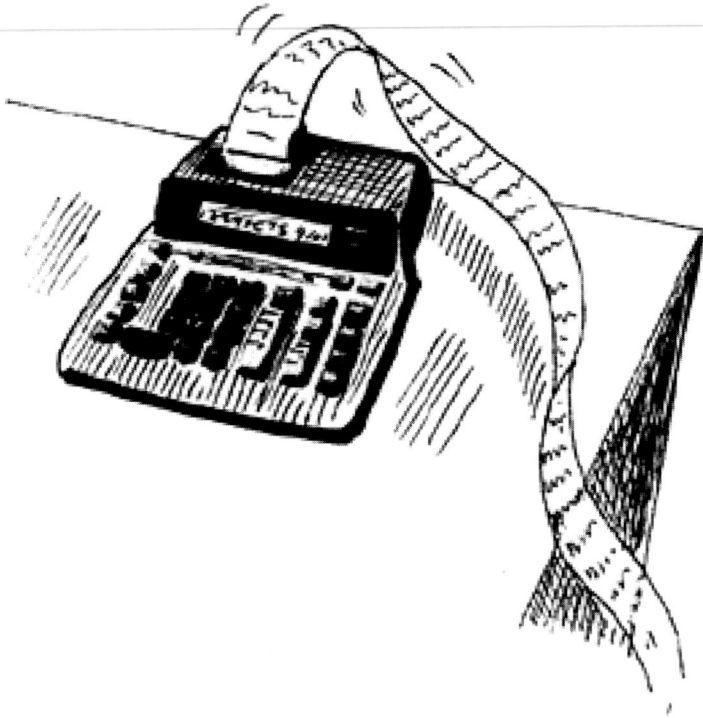

These days success or failure is built on small profit margins. All employees have to help the business grow.

To keep a job, one must contribute to the growth of his employer's business.

COMMON SENSE and HARD WORK will lead to SUCCESS!

*Personal
Development*

Mr. Sanders had to fire Alvin because he was indifferent and he had a chip on his shoulder. He also chased customers away. Rate yourself on the traits you think you have by placing an X on the appropriate line.

	HIGH	MEDIUM	LOW
A responsible worker	____	____	____
Listens to instructions	____	____	____
A dependable worker	____	____	____
Follows directions	____	____	____
A willing worker	____	____	____
Takes the initiative	____	____	____
A loyal employee	____	____	____
Possess a positive attitude	____	____	____
An honest worker	____	____	____

Questions you might be asked on the interview:

1. Why do you want to work?
2. Tell me something about your background.
3. What type of education and technical training have you had?
4. Describe a typical workday with your previous employer.
5. Name your greatest contribution to your previous employer.
6. What part-time jobs have you had and why did you leave?
7. Name three references and tell me what each might say about you.
8. Can you prepare a written report?

KEEPING A JOB

Crossword Puzzle
The answers to this puzzle may be found within the starburst on the previous page.

Across
3. reliable, involving obligations or duties
6. fair and upright
7. cheerfully ready
8. following these will keep you from getting lost

Down
1. orders
2. a person you can rely on for support or help is this
4. one who takes the lead shows this
5. true and faithful to promise or duty

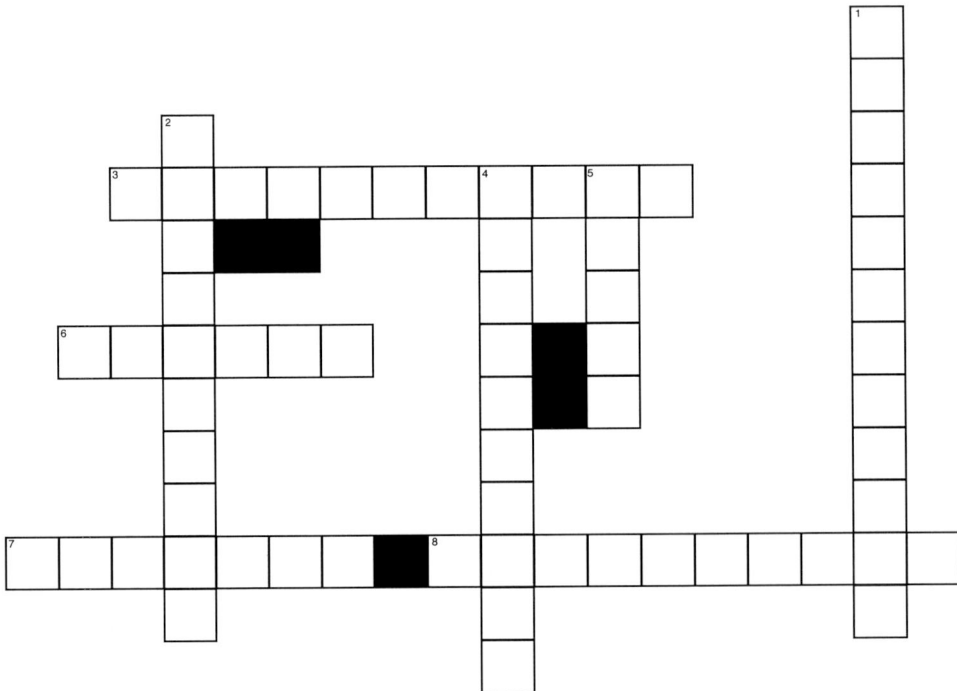

Answers can be found on page 56.

ANSWER KEY

COMMUNICATION SKILLS & NON-VERBAL COMMUNICATION

COMPLETE THE SENTENCES

1. mental drifting
2. listening
3. knowledge
4. 25 seconds
5. think ahead, central theme, evaluate
6. practice
7. retain
8. notes
9. speaking tone
10. vocabulary

MATCHING

1. d
2. e
3. a
4. b
5. c

TRUE OR FALSE

1. T
2. T
3. F
4. T
5. T

ANSWER KEY

PROBLEM SOLVING

SENTENCE COMPLETION

1. can
2. series
3. recognize
4. fact, opinion
5. practice

TRUE OR FALSE

1. T
2. T
3. T
4. T
5. T
6. T
7. T
8. T

ANSWER KEY

GETTING A JOB

SENTENCE COMPLETION

1. yourself
2. interests
3. search, newspapers, friends
4. interview, resumé
5. income, benefits

JOB PARTS

1. Self-knowledge
2. The job search
3. The interview

THE JOB SEARCH

1. Newspapers, State Employment Office, Civil Service Office, High School Counselor, Job Placement Counselor

2. Review your job folder, shower, dress well, leave early to get to the interview on time

3. Chew gum
   Answer your cell phone
   Bite your fingernails
   Smoke
   Have a bad attitude
   Yawn
   Tell a bad joke
   Look discouraged
   Comb your hair
   Put on lipstick
   Be a wise guy

ANSWER KEY

KEEPING A JOB

CROSSWORD PUZZLE

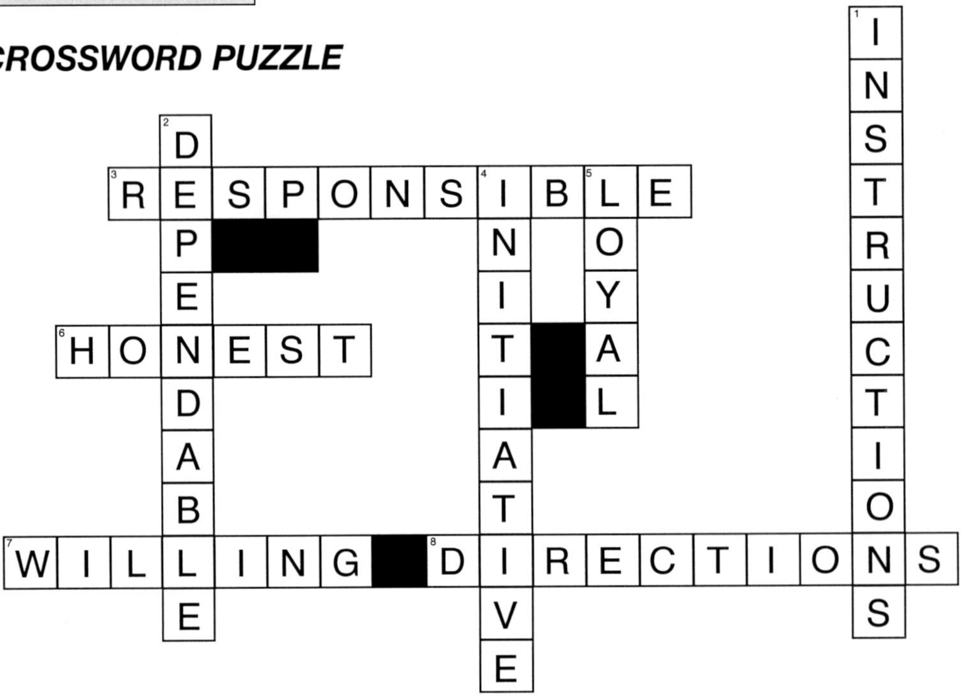

1 INSTRUCTIONS
2 DEPENDABLE
3 RESPONSIBLE
4 INITIATIVE
5 LOYAL
6 HONEST
7 WILLING
8 DIRECTIONS